Contents

GW00600681

The Philippines

Politics and military power

Introduction

In many countries of the Third World, newly democratic regimes are held hostage by still-powerful armies inherited from dictatorship. The military, intolerant of dissent and refusing to be weaned from its practice of political intervention, limits the manoeuvring room for civilian elites to implement social reforms and restricts the democratic space in which popular movements can organise and struggle for change. The Philippines is no exception to this pattern.

In February 1986 hundreds of thousands of Filipinos poured onto the streets of the Philippine capital of Manila to back a revolt by a section of the armed forces against dictator Ferdinand Marcos. 'People power' tipped the balance in favour of Corazon ('Cory') Aquino who was sworn in as president, having been fraudulently robbed of victory in elections held the same month.

Many Filipinos expected that the 'people power revolution' would bring real reforms and genuine democracy to a country that had been ravaged by 14 years of dictatorship. But six years after the fall of Marcos these hopes have vanished. President Aquino has been unable to implement major socio-economic reforms and the democratic institutions she has established are constantly threatened by a politicised military that has attempted to grab power six times in as many years.

2

Aquino's term ends in May 1992 when Filipinos will have their first real election in 20 years. Sadly this election could pave the way for the return of a Marcos-style government. Imelda Marcos, the dictator's flamboyant wife, is seeking the presidency, as is Eduardo 'Danding' Cojuangco Jr, Aquino's first cousin, who was Marcos' foremost business supporter. In a country where elections have traditionally been fought on the basis of fraud, intimidation and financial inducement, the remnants of the Marcos era are being given another chance to wield power.

The Armed Forces of the Philippines (AFP) are supposed to play a neutral role during elections. But military officers have traditionally taken sides, terrorising voters or committing fraud in support of politicians. The military has always been tied to political elites who ensure pay-offs and promotions for favoured officers.

Historically, Filipino elites have been composed of powerful clans, linked through patronage, whose wealth derives from monopoly control over land, internal trade and commerce, extraction of natural resources and gambling, or partnership with foreign capital. They have used the armed forces to protect their interests and quell grassroots resistance to elite rule. Since the 1930s soldiers have put down peasant rebellions and, in much of the Philippine countryside, the military man is still seen as the defender and protector of landed interests.

The fourth force

Before Marcos gave the AFP more money and power, military officers were content to be the beneficiaries of elite patronage and did not aspire to wield power themselves; they were quite happy to leave the problems of government to politicians. But one of the most enduring legacies of the Marcos dictatorship is a powerful and politicised military which behaves like an independent branch of government, often resisting civilian control. Although democratic institutions have been formally restored, the armed forces continue to wield tremendous power and remain one of the most formidable obstacles to Philippine democratisation.

Six years of democracy have not substantially diminished the size, budget or power of the AFP; nor have they ended military corruption and abuses. The AFP are today the sole custodian of counterinsurgency policy. A communist rebellion has raged in the

Philippines for more than 20 years, finding support among landless peasants, discontented workers and the disillusioned middle class. The AFP have waged an often brutal campaign against the rebellion and its suspected sympathisers, including legitimate dissenters and women and children living in rural villages. By the end of 1991, it was estimated that military operations, including heavy bombing of villages suspected of forming part of the communist mass base, had displaced two million people. Civilian officials have been unable to rein in the over-zealous armed forces. Even though the principle of civilian supremacy is enshrined in the Constitution, the fear of military unrest has paralysed the Aquino government's efforts to control the armed forces and prosecute cases of human rights abuse, even those which took place under Marcos.

In fact, the military often vetoes civilian officials, particularly in the area of defence policy. Moreover, military and defence officials encroach on areas of government that are properly the turf of civilians. Retired generals head key government agencies. Military officers publicly criticise government policy and openly lobby the government on issues like the extension of the lease on US military bases in the Philippines.

Since invasion by the United States at the turn of the century, the Philippines has been a major outpost for US military power. The United States used its bases in the Philippines as staging points for US intervention in the Korean and Vietnam wars, for example. And the AFP, because they are dependent on US military assistance, have acted as the guarantor of US interests in the country. In recent negotiations on the future of US troops in the Philippines, the armed forces were a formidable lobby for a continued US military presence.

The institutions of formal democracy were established in the Philippines at the end of the Second World War when the country became independent from the United States. A US-style presidential system of government was set up with a constitution modelled on that of the United States. As in the United States, two political parties not substantially different from each other alternated in power. The political system, however, while formally democratic, was essentially elitist. For most of the postwar period, political office was dominated by the landowning elite which remained in power through elections fought with money, violence and patronage.

Marcos, a provincial politician who rose to power through the clever manipulation of elite politics, removed all trappings of democracy when he declared martial law in 1972. Backed by the United States, which retained a powerful influence in its former colony, Marcos was able to consolidate his control over the AFP and used this power against both rival elites and grassroots opposition, including the nascent communist rebellion.

By 1986, however, Marcos had lost the support of both the military and the United States and it was this factor, combined with popular discontent, which led to his downfall. A dissident military faction led by Juan Ponce Enrile, the ambitious defence minister, moved to take power from the ailing dictator; it was the discovery of this plot which triggered the military-backed uprising that ended with the fall of Marcos.

For many military officers, however, the events of February 1986 were taken as a justification for the belief that the armed forces can and should be a leading political actor, and ushered in a period of military interventionism. Indeed, the six attempted coups since the 1986 'revolution' have been premised on the argument that since the armed forces played a key role in bringing Aquino to power, her government existed only on the military's sufferance. A 1987 survey showed that about a third of AFP officers believed that the military had the right to use force to unseat an incompetent head of state. Nearly half of those polled said the armed forces should temporarily take over government to prevent a communist victory.

Ironically, Aquino, like Marcos before her, has relied on the loyalty of the main military factions and the support of the United States in order to continue in power. The coup attempts have failed largely because of the support of loyal officers, led by her former chief of staff, General Fidel Ramos, and of successive US governments. Aquino, however, has paid a political cost for such support. Within two years of taking power, her 'revolutionary government' had become conservative and pro-American.

US influence and counterinsurgency

The Philippine military was created in the image of its US counterpart. The AFP's training and orientation, even their drills and manuals, are cloned from the US Army. The Philippine Military

Academy, the elite training ground of the AFP officer corps, is modelled on West Point.

The AFP were, from the beginning, designed mainly for counterinsurgency, with the United States playing a major role in directing and financing counterinsurgency strategy and efforts. By propping up US-supported elites, the armed forces have helped preserve a feudalistic society where land and power are the monopoly of a few families and have often dealt harshly with individuals and popular movements that question US influence and elite rule. Their worldview sees the elite-dominated social order as natural and good for society.

The AFP's origins can be traced back to the turn of the century when the United States, then an emerging world power in search of a base in the Pacific, defeated Spain in the 1898 Spanish-American War and subsequently invaded the Philippines which had been a Spanish colony since the 16th century. In the Philippine-American War between 1898 and 1902, over 70,000 US troops were sent to the Philippines and up to 300,000 Filipinos died in the fight for independence. As part of its efforts to crush Filipino resistance, in 1901 the United States created the Insular Police Force with 74 US officers who formed and trained the Philippine Scouts, a mercenary unit of native soldiers who fought with US troops to suppress guerrilla activity and 'pacify' the islands. In 1917 the Insular Police Force became the Philippine Constabulary which was to become the core of the Philippine armed forces.

Following the inauguration in 1935 of the Philippine Commonwealth — a transition government during which Filipinos were supposed to prepare for self-rule under US tutelage — US General Douglas MacArthur was named the government's chief military adviser and asked to draw up a defence plan for the Philippines. The United States thus played a major part in defining the Philippine armed forces' role, limiting the AFP to internal security and making the Philippines formally reliant on the United States for external defence.

Because the US government financed the AFP's organisation, it also defined the armed forces' size, budget, training, equipment and supplies. The AFP remain dependent on US military assistance for equipment, logistics and training. In turn, such assistance is contingent on the continued presence of US military bases in the

Philippines. Since 1986, the Philippines has received about US$100 million a year in US military aid.

The Philippines became independent in 1946. But the Philippine armed forces were not involved in the independence struggle and military officers were not thrust into prominent political roles as they were in other Asian countries. Independence was negotiated between Washington and the Manila elite. The United States proudly paraded the Philippines as a showcase of US-style democracy. In reality, however, this meant that the Philippines, in exchange for formal independence, agreed to host US troops and to allow US citizens equal rights to exploit Philippine resources.

The AFP were at that time subordinated to civilian authority and remained a background presence of national life. Only in the 1950s, when a peasant rebellion raged in central Luzon, were the AFP pushed into the limelight. The *Hukbalahap* (People's Anti-Japanese Army), allied with the old Communist Party, fought the Japanese during the Second World War. After the war, the Huks gained support among landless peasants in Central Luzon and by the early 1950s posed a serious threat to the Manila government.

The fight against the Huk insurgents was led by Defence Secretary Ramon Magsaysay whose strategy, known as *armor con amor*, combined military might and social and economic development programmes. The brains behind Magsaysay's campaign was Lt Col Edward Lansdale, who worked for an advertising company before he joined US military intelligence and then the Central Intelligence Agency (CIA). Lansdale would later claim that he invented Magsaysay. The CIA's counterinsurgency tactics included psychological warfare operations which featured soldiers snatching the last man in a Huk patrol in the jungles and puncturing his neck with two holes, draining his blood and leaving his corpse on the trail. The soldiers then spread the word that vampires were on the prowl against the Huks, thus terrorising Huk sympathisers in the villages.

Magsaysay's successful campaign against the Huks thrust him into the presidency in 1953. As president, he institutionalised the AFP's involvement in civic action and socio-economic programmes, like the building of schools and roads and the provision of medical and legal assistance to poor villages. While the AFP's role was expanded to include non-military functions, the armed forces rarely intervened directly in actual government.

Anxious to advance their careers, however, military officers routinely sought patrons among elite politicians in Congress. As promotions from the rank of colonel had to be approved by a congressional commission, military officers relied on the sponsorship of politicians for promotion. The Philippines is held together by a web of patron-client relations and the armed forces are no exception. Such client ties would be revealed during elections when officers loyal to a particular candidate deployed their troops to terrorise their patron's rivals. Military officers would often be on the payroll of politicians, providing them with security and other services, including the intimidation of dissenters. The military thus came to be used not so much to protect the interests of the state but of the elites controlling the state. To this day, soldiers and paramilitary troopers are assigned to guard mines, plantations and forests controlled by politicians.

Following the election of Marcos as president in 1965, the use of the AFP as a political tool and their role in counterinsurgency became even more pronounced. Marcos made the AFP an integral part of his social and economic development strategy, mobilising the armed forces for infrastructure, health and community self-help programmes on a far greater scale than Magsaysay ever did. The AFP supervised the building of roads, schools and irrigation systems and became involved in land resettlement and the planning and construction of industrial sites. This expansion of the military's role was actively encouraged by the United States. In fact, Marcos followed to the letter a blueprint for the AFP's civic action programme prepared by the US State Department.

In his first 13 months in office, Marcos himself headed the Defence Department. To prepare the armed forces for their new role, he refurbished and expanded the AFP's educational institutions and encouraged the training of military officers in management skills. With US support, thousands of Philippine military officers were sent for advanced training in US schools. Marcos also substantially increased the AFP's size and budget. And, much more than any previous Philippine president, he built up his own base of support, through patronage, within the armed forces. In the biggest reshuffle in Philippine military history, he changed nearly half of the officers in the military top brass, replacing them with men who were personally loyal to him.

The Marcos era

By the late 1960s, Philippine society was in crisis, as the old patronage-based party system wilted under the strain of the growing demands placed on it. Since the 1940s the Philippines had been governed by politicians representing the landowning class who contested elective posts through two parties which alternated in office. There was little to distinguish between the parties and their main goal was to frustrate social reforms and keep the elite in power. Through the years, the parties monopolised public office by maintaining a hierarchical system of patronage. Local politicians dealt out money, jobs and public-works projects to their communities in exchange for electoral support. In turn, these politicians were dependent on congressional patronage. Congress managed so-called 'pork barrel funds', allocations for public-works projects which they gave out to local leaders who helped them get elected.

By the time Marcos became president, economic modernisation was already undermining the loyalties on which the patron-client networks of politicians were based. The entry of new groups into the political process — the middle class as well as politicised student, worker and peasant groups — created new pressures on the political system. Urbanisation and migration to the cities led to a weakening of feudalistic ties to local leaders and economic difficulties made people increasingly cynical of politicians and the elite. Elections became increasingly fraudulent and violent, as the old client networks could no longer be relied upon to deliver the votes. At the same time, rivalry among the elites over the control of state resources intensified.

In 1969 Marcos won a second presidential term in one of the bloodiest and most fraud-marred elections in Philippine history. Marcos was a calculating and scheming politician and his ambitions were matched only by his ruthlessness. The expansion of the armed forces and their performance of non-military functions were part of the preparations for dictatorship. Banned by the constitution from seeking a third term, Marcos laid the groundwork for martial law by using patronage to consolidate his hold over the armed forces to an unprecedented degree.

With the military behind him, Marcos succeeded in sweeping aside constitutional restraints to his continued rule. Taking

9

advantage of student unrest and increasing radicalism in the cities and countryside, Marcos suspended the writ of habeas corpus in 1971, allowing himself the power to arrest activists and political enemies without a warrant. And in September 1972, he declared martial law in consultation with a dozen advisers, known as the 'Rolex 12' because they each received a Rolex watch from Marcos. All but two of the advisers were high-ranking, active-duty military officers.

Martial law

By declaring martial law and suspending the constitution, Marcos outmanoeuvred rival politicians who wanted their turn to run the country. Congress was abolished, demonstrations were banned, political parties were outlawed and civil and political rights were suspended. Newspapers and broadcast stations that had been Asia's freest media were closed, with some eventually allowed to reopen under a regime of strict censorship. Thousands were hauled off to jail, including rival politicians and businessmen, student activists, peasant and worker organisers, and suspected communists. In the first five years of martial law 70,000 people were jailed for political offences. The torture of political prisoners became the military's standard practice. Hundreds were summarily executed while others became part of the long list of 'missing' or 'disappeared'.

Many of the officers appointed to top posts by Marcos came from his native Ilocos region. He pampered them and gave them a lifestyle which previously only politicians had enjoyed. Moreover, by abolishing Congress and personally naming local officials, Marcos centralised patronage in the office of the president. In place of the network of civilian officials, Marcos courted patronage through military officers who began to enjoy unprecedented power and privilege. Whereas people had previously sought out politicians for jobs, dole-outs and public-works projects, after martial law they began approaching military officers instead. And the armed forces, while taking over patronage-dispensing functions from the politicians, were themselves dependent on their supreme patron, Marcos.

Marcos further tightened his hold over the armed forces by financially rewarding the AFP for their role as the chief implementor of martial law. From 1972 to 1977 the defence budget grew nearly ten-fold from 608 million pesos to P5.4 billion and by the 1970s military expenditures had displaced education as the top item in the national budget. The size of the AFP doubled from 53,000 in 1971 to 113,000 in 1976, with the number of AFP regular forces reaching their peak in 1985 at 158,300. Marcos also beefed up the paramilitary forces, comprised mainly of villagers who were paid only a third of enlisted men's wages to act as guides and assistants to regular troops and often used as cannon fodder in the intensifying war with communist guerrillas. In the late 1970s 25,000 men were recruited to join paramilitary units, rising by 1985 to 65,000. Previously under the control of local officials, the police were integrated into military ranks, thus centralising law-enforcement functions under the AFP command.

Marcos justified the expansion of the armed forces as necessary to cope with the burgeoning communist and Muslim rebellions. Soon after martial law was declared, Muslim secessionists, aided by Libya and other Islamic countries, staged major offensives in the southern island of Mindanao. The AFP retaliated in kind. In four years, until a truce was called in 1976, nearly one million Filipinos were displaced in the fighting.

In 1968 university-educated youth teamed up with the peasant remnants of the Huk rebellion to form the new Communist Party of the Philippines (CPP). In 1969, the CPP went on to turn a rag-tag band of guerrillas into the New People's Army (NPA). The NPA grew rapidly, its expansion fanned by the excesses of the Marcos regime and the abuses of the military. The rebels also attracted significant numbers of middle-class youths disgruntled with the dictatorship but prevented by martial law from engaging in open dissent. By the early 1980s the NPA numbered almost 20,000 guerrillas and was even gaining the grudging respect of the traditionally conservative middle and upper classes.

Factionalism and the AFP's changing role

Marcos also expanded military functions to include not only counterinsurgency and civic action but actual government tasks. Overnight, military officers became bureaucrats, business executives, judges and politicians and were put in charge of public utilities, government agencies and state corporations. Officers took on overtly political roles, becoming provincial governors in a few areas. In addition, military courts tried political offences.

By expanding their size, budget and functions, Marcos drastically changed the nature and outlook of the armed forces. Intoxicated with its new powers and perquisites, the military elite became a willing instrument of the dictatorship and acquired a new confidence about its capacity to tackle non-military functions. By 1974 several generals were already claiming that martial law had given the AFP an awareness of their ability to run the government.

This sense of self-esteem, however, was not warranted by the military's record. By the 1980s complaints of military corruption were rife: generals and colonels had become notorious for driving around in limousines, living in palatial houses and escorting expensive mistresses. While the top brass enriched themselves, the soldiers in the field suffered from lack of supplies, decrepit equipment and inadequate training. Institutionally, the armed forces became increasingly factionalised as Marcos sought to maintain his grip over the bloated military he had created by giving strategic postings to loyal officers, led by his cousin and chief of staff, General Fabian Ver.

Ver began as Marcos's driver and aide, working his way up to become head of the Presidential Security Command, a pampered unit whose sole concern was the safety of the Marcos family. In August 1981 Ver was named armed forces chief of staff, an appointment that upset the AFP promotions system and caused great disaffection in the officer corps. The move also angered other pretenders to Marcos's throne like the ambitious defence minister, Juan Ponce Enrile. For nearly a decade Enrile had been the chief administrator of martial law and the second most powerful Philippine official after Marcos. But by the late 1970s Marcos saw him as a threat and began to cut back his power. For his part, Enrile interpreted Ver's appointment as AFP chief of staff as a sign that Marcos was paving the way for his wife Imelda's succession to the presidency.

As a counterbalance, Enrile cultivated the loyalties of other officers, most of them majors and colonels in the defence ministry. In 1981 Enrile's men began to import weapons and train, partly in self-defence, as Enrile believed that Ver would eventually plot to kill him. The defence minister also began consolidating his forces as he was increasingly being outmanoeuvred by Ver. The officers close to Enrile would later form the core group of the Reform the Armed Forces Movement (RAM) which attempted to stage a coup against Marcos and which would also seek, on several occasions, to topple Aquino.

In the end, however, the powerful and factionalised military Marcos had created would trigger his downfall.

The battle for succession

As the end of the Marcos regime neared and the battle for his succession seemed imminent, palace intrigues became more vicious. Ver and Imelda Marcos began consolidating the Marcos loyalists in the AFP. At the same time, Enrile stepped up preparations for a post-Marcos era and by 1985 RAM was openly recruiting members throughout the country. The AFP factions were not ideological. Despite their different patrons, they were homogeneous in their staunch anti-communism, their belief in powerful and politically interventionist armed forces, and their support for the status quo of elite rule and US influence. RAM's major grievance was favouritism in the armed forces. Although RAM members were critical of military excesses, many were themselves involved in torture and were the corrupt beneficiaries of patronage — not from Ver or Marcos but from Enrile.

The Marcos dictatorship was propped up in no small measure by the US government and the international financial system which poured billions of dollars in aid and loans into the Philippines. Much of the money was siphoned off into Marcos' Swiss bank accounts or used to buy Manhattan real estate and finance the flamboyant projects of Imelda Marcos. The United States was nevertheless prepared to defend the Marcos regime against domestic and international criticism.

US military assistance also kept the armed forces afloat and made them a more effective tool of dictatorship. In 1972, the first year of martial law, US military aid totalled US$50 million — more than one-third of the Philippine defence budget — and increased sharply until 1983, when it tapered off following the assassination of Cory Aquino's husband Benigno, a former opposition senator and Marcos' political arch-rival.

It was widely believed that the top military brass, under orders from Marcos or his wife, was responsible for Benigno Aquino's murder. The killing marked the beginning of the end of Marcos: it unleashed widespread popular protest and set the middle and upper classes, the powerful Catholic Church hierarchy and sections of the US government against the regime. It also led to further informal contact between disgruntled military officers who later formed RAM.

RAM's rhetoric of military reform attracted young idealistic officers worried about the corrupt and divided state of the armed forces. It also drew the support of disaffected officers whose careers did not prosper because they were outside Ver's clique. The chief of staff, who was not a graduate of the elite Philippine Military Academy (PMA), preferred to name non-PMA officers to important posts. This caused considerable resentment among officers who had graduated from the Academy, from which the top brass was traditionally recruited.

RAM's organisation was based on the PMA student network and its success was due partly to the strong fraternal bonds that existed between former classmates. The core group of RAM, composed of graduates from the Academy in 1971, including Lt Cols Gregorio Honasan, Eduardo Kapunan and Victor Batac, represented the martial-law generation of military officers. As lieutenants, they were sent to the countryside to fight communist rebels or Muslim insurgents.

Early in their careers, the officers of the RAM leadership were exposed to the inner workings of power. Assigned as aides to powerful political figures like Enrile, they enjoyed the perquisites that accompanied such associations and learned to deal with a wide cross-section of people, acquiring political skills and contacts that were unusual for Filipino military officers. In mid-1985 the RAM core group secretly began plans for a coup against Marcos. Publicly, the organisation continued to press for military reforms, recruit members and meet with civilians. RAM members met with Church groups and representatives of Cory Aquino's campaign for the forthcoming presidential elections, including her brother, Jose 'Peping' Cojuangco Jr, and businessman Jaime Ongpin, a key election strategist and a major financial backer of her candidacy. Cleverly using the media, RAM built up a credible public image even as it was clandestinely plotting a coup.

RAM timed its coup attempt to take advantage of popular disenchantment with Marcos following Aquino's fraudulent defeat in the election. When the plot was discovered, Filipinos were already on the verge of an uprising. As the conspirators made a last stand in a military camp in Manila, the camp became the focus of anger against Marcos. Thousands descended on the area to protest, standing between the opposing AFP factions. Realising that Marcos' end was near, the soldiers deserted the forces loyal to the dictator in droves and refused to fire on the crowds. Disowned by his people, the AFP and the United States, Marcos and his family were forced to flee the country in a US Army helicopter. Aquino became president, the first Filipino head of state to be swept to power on a wave of popular euphoria.

Aquino and military pressure

Aquino inherited a politicised and divided military which was suspicious of civilians and jealous of its powers. Aquino and her advisers initially refused to make any concessions to the armed forces but, as the military became more restive, they began to surrender more and more power. This, however, did not calm the rebelliousness among the top brass and the barracks. Despite the restoration of democratic institutions — a popularly ratified constitution, a Congress and a free press — the government faced the constant threat of military upheaval.

Aquino's relationship with the AFP was rocky from the very beginning. Because the armed forces played an important part in the uprising, they demanded a major influence over government policy. In her first week as president, Aquino upset the top brass when she honoured an election campaign promise to release all political prisoners, including alleged high-ranking CPP leaders.

In the following months, the armed forces strongly opposed the government's decision to declare a cease-fire and hold peace talks with the communist rebels represented by the broader umbrella organisation, the National Democratic Front (NDF). Military officials became increasingly concerned that they might lose control of counterinsurgency policy to civilians. Moreover, the government's intention to investigate military abuses personally threatened key officers, including the RAM leaders, whose past record of involvement in torture and summary executions would almost certainly be disclosed.

Plots and Concessions

In media interviews, RAM members articulated the grievances of many in the military who felt that Aquino was swayed by 'leftist' advisers and human-rights lawyers who were now cabinet ministers. They were supported by conservative sectors of the US government. The US Defence Department made no secret of its view that Aquino's policy of reconciliation with the communist rebels was naive and dangerous, as did the CIA. A US journalist reported that, by the last quarter of 1986, the CIA station chief in Manila had concluded that Aquino's policy toward the communists threatened US interests and that the Philippine military should be encouraged to topple her. Emboldened by their knowledge of US support, RAM members plotted to overthrow Aquino. But they were dissuaded from pursuing their plans by chief of staff General Fidel Ramos who sympathised with the movement's grievances but preferred a more gradualist approach.

To appease the military, Aquino agreed to place a time limit on the duration of the cease-fire, fire two ministers accused of being communist sympathisers and tone down human-rights investigations. But the armed forces were not satisfied. In August 1987 and December 1989 RAM mobilised thousands of troops in coup attempts that came very close to toppling the government.

Under Aquino the armed forces became even more factionalised than under Marcos. The old patronage networks remained intact, with officers remaining loyal to the politicians who had nurtured them during the dictatorship. A significant corps of officers also remained fanatically loyal to Marcos, engineering small-scale rebellions which fizzled out. These included taking over army camps, television stations and even the de luxe Manila Hotel. The core of RAM continued to support Enrile and, through their attempted coups in 1986 and 1987, sought to make him head of state. Although the RAM leadership pursued Enrile's ambitions, it also mobilised many officers who opposed Aquino's initially conciliatory stance towards the communist rebellion and the progressive social reforms advocated by some of her advisers. As in the February 1986 coup plot against Marcos, RAM was able to tap discontent within the officer corps.

RAM raised the same grievances against Aquino as they had against Marcos — favouritism in the military, corruption and factionalism. In the December 1989 coup attempt, RAM even teamed up with Marcos loyalists in the military, their alliance based on a common hatred of Aquino. For its part, the pro-Aquino faction in the military led by AFP chief of staff General Ramos tried to win the loyalty of officers by promising promotions and key posts, thus creating its own network of patronage.

As during the Marcos era, the military factions under Aquino reflected the divisions among the ruling elite rather than ideological differences. The AFP remained a staunch defender of elite rule and US domination, united in their suspicion of civilian officials and confident of their ability to rule; their worldview continued to be deeply conservative, obsessed with the elimination of communism (which actually meant any form of opposition to the status quo). Indeed, the military routinely crushed peasants and workers who, emboldened by the 1986 uprising, began to carry out dramatic protest actions like the occupation of land abandoned by Marcos cronies. Soldiers continued to guard mines, plantations and prawn farms against dissenters. Thus, although Aquino became president under the slogan of 'people power', the armed forces' repression of above ground movements advocating radical social reforms thwarted the extension of democracy and the redistribution of wealth.

As ambitious military factions continued to plot against her government, Aquino made more and more concessions, increasing the defence budget, granting a hefty rise in soldiers' pay and giving military officers a stronger voice in government. She pardoned officers who joined the coup attempts, even if they openly continued to defy her government, and sacked most of the progressive ministers who had fought for social reforms.

The repression of 'democratic space'

As a result of the reshuffles that followed each attempted coup, the Aquino cabinet became increasingly homogeneous in ideological terms, with a heavy slant towards bankers, businessmen, technocrats and retired military officers. The coup attempts have enabled the armed forces to act like the fourth branch of government, effectively vetoing the executive, the legislature and even the judiciary, especially over crucial policies like counterinsurgency. Aquino allowed the military to continue the 'dirty war' begun by Marcos. The government's negotiations with communist and Muslim rebels collapsed and, within a year, the government's initial commitment to human rights had been eroded.

The military's patience with the open dissent encouraged by democracy began wearing thin. In January 1987 government security forces fired on a rally of thousands of farmers demanding land reform outside the presidential palace, killing 18. The massacre prompted communist negotiators to end the peace talks. Soon afterwards, Aquino surrendered to military pressure for 'all-out war' against communism and gave the AFP a virtual carte blanche to bomb villages accused of sympathising with the guerrillas. She also gave her blessing to the activities of anti-communist vigilantes who killed suspected NPA rebels on sight, occasionally beheading them. Military and vigilante terror forced millions out of their homes and villages, part of a counterinsurgency strategy aimed at depriving guerrillas of their perceived mass base. The worst hit by this strategy, however, were not the guerrillas but peasant and tribal children, hundreds of whom have died of disease in cramped and unsafe evacuation centres to which their families had fled. In the last three years, these military operations have killed more children than rebels.

The forced evacuations have created a floating population uprooted from their native villages and unable to settle elsewhere. In many areas, these displacements have destroyed community organisations and basic Christian communities that had been painstakingly built over many years, successfully improving people's livelihoods and enabling them to stand up to local elites and military commanders. Such resistance, however, has made these communities suspect in the AFP's eyes. Communities which assert themselves are immediately branded communist and suffer the military's ire.

The anti-communist hysteria whipped up by the military greatly diminished the 'democratic space' that was one of the main achievements of the 'people power revolution'. Aquino had restored press freedom and allowed groups from across the ideological spectrum to organise openly. But the military witch-hunt restricted these freedoms. Individuals, including high government officials, and groups advocating radical policies like land reform, the removal of US military bases and the repudiation of foreign debt were immediately branded communist. A left-wing political party, *Partido ng Bayan* (People's Party), which put forward candidates in the 1987 congressional elections, was severely persecuted and several of its leaders were killed, forcing the party into semi-clandestine existence.

Advocacy groups and grassroots organisations were particularly vulnerable to harassment, as the AFP's emphasis on dismantling the 'political infrastructure' of the rebellion — a network of legal groups supposedly fronting for the CPP — made all dissenters open to suspicion. In the last six years a whole array of people — lawyers, priests, environmental activists, journalists and human-rights workers — have been imprisoned or killed because of their alleged communist leanings. These suspicions were often unwarranted, with the military acting to protect elite interests against any form of challenge.

The AFP remained intimately tied to their elite patrons and, throughout the Philippines, military officers continued to provide protection for logging and mining companies, plantations, prawn farms and local politicians.

In Negros for example, where sugar planters and millers dominate political and economic life, a determined military campaign to crush the communist movement was sponsored by sugar plantation owners who armed and funded paramilitary units in order to reinforce regular troops. Encouraged by landowners, the military pursued radical trade unionists who had politicised sugarcane workers and, in several areas, had helped them to introduce their own land reform by taking over lands foreclosed by banks or abandoned by Marcos cronies. The bombing of villages and summary execution of trade unionists dismantled workers' organisations and set back efforts in favour of land reform.

The Catholic and Protestant churches have been at the forefront of protests against military abuses. But, as under Marcos, this has only made them the target of military persecution. Many churchpeople have been imprisoned and killed since 1986.

Patronage and discontent

With the restoration of Congress, politicians again became the main dispensers of patronage, although the formidable clout still wielded by the military also allowed officers to play this role. The revival of the congressional commission approving military promotions meant that officers had to court the favour of politicians. Politicians like Aquino's brother, José 'Peping' Cojuangco Jr, a congressman who is secretary of the ruling *Lakas ng Demokratikong Pilipino* (LDP) party, pampered coteries within the armed forces. Aquino herself named loyal generals to lucrative government posts, such as the Customs Commission, a traditional source of graft, and the Philippine Gaming and Amusement Corporation, which supervises gambling casinos. She also appointed retired generals to head crucial government agencies like the Department of National Defence and the National Intelligence Co-ordinating Agency. Chief of staff Ramos built his own patronage base within the AFP, parcelling out plum postings in exchange for the loyalty of favoured officers.

The Aquino-Ramos network of patronage matched, though to a much lesser degree, the Marcos-Ver network. It alienated officers excluded from the clique who became ripe for recruitment by RAM which sought to deepen disaffection with the government by exploiting charges of ineptness and corruption against high officials, including Aquino relatives. As Aquino's popularity dipped, partly due to her government's inability to address pressing social problems and deliver basic public services, the military became more restive. Disenchanted officers were courted by anti-Aquino politicians like Enrile, Vice-President Salvador Laurel and Eduardo 'Danding' Cojuangco Jr. Thus RAM interests became intertwined with those of anti-government elites.

Under Aquino, however, RAM rhetoric has undergone a transformation. Virulently anti-communist and pro-US in origin, RAM began issuing populist and nationalist statements after its failed coup attempts in December 1989 when the US government sent Phantom jets to help pro-Aquino troops put down the rebellion. Although the US planes were not crucial in logistical terms, RAM claimed they dealt the movement a crippling psychological blow — officers committed to the coup backed out when they discovered that US forces were supporting the government. Since then, the movement has criticised the United States for supporting Aquino and has changed its name to *Rebolusyunaryong Alyansang Makabayan* (Revolutionary Nationalist Alliance), with the same acronym, RAM.

RAM leaders have always had close links with Pentagon and CIA officials in the Philippines and this contact made the movement confident that it would eventually win Washington's support for a military junta. After all, US support for Marcos had taught RAM that the United States would support a repressive, military-dominated government so long as it protected US interests.

US support

RAM, however, failed to appreciate that by 1989 Aquino was an effective guarantor of US interests. She had declared total war against the communists; her cabinet had been purged of alleged leftists; and government policies were veering increasingly rightwards. US interests were better served by a conservative, legitimately elected government than by a military-installed junta, no matter how pro-American.

RAM also underestimated the degree to which the United States was prepared to intervene directly in the Philippines. As in 1987, it thought that the United States would merely issue rhetorical statements condemning the coup and supporting Aquino. But it did not: upon Aquino's request US President Bush ordered US planes at a US base near Manila to provide cover for Philippine government pilots attacking RAM aircraft. This was the first time that the United States had used an overseas military base to defend a host government. Three weeks later, the Americans invaded Panama, the first time an overseas US military base was used to overthrow the host government.

The United States remains a profound influence on the Philippine armed forces and US military assistance is the lifeline of the AFP. This support is tied to the US military bases and if American troops leave the Philippines, US aid is bound to be drastically cut. Since 1986, the AFP has received an average of US$100 million a year from Washington and without this assistance the armed forces will have to look elsewhere for equipment, supplies and training. From 1950 to the mid-1980s 15,000 AFP officers were trained in the United States which provides the Philippines with the bulk of its armoury.

The removal of US aid will further impoverish the AFP which, despite US support, are poorly equipped. They have no anti-armour, anti-aircraft or anti-ship missiles and existing equipment is obsolete: their reconditioned helicopters are prone to malfunctions and crashes. The Philippine military is in such a sorry state partly because the United States has discouraged the AFP from building up their own independent defence capability. Washington has at times even barred the Philippines from purchasing military equipment from countries other than the United States.

The AFP are still one of the staunchest advocates of the US presence. But such a position pits the armed forces against a growing number of Filipinos who are against the bases. And within the AFP themselves, junior officers are beginning to question the US presence. In 1988 the Young Officers' Union (YOU) was clandestinely formed. Composed mainly of lieutenants and majors, YOU is very critical of the United States and of the elite. But the group's real size and influence remain unknown.

To a lesser extent, RAM, too, has become anti-US. But the depth of its anti-Americanism has yet to be proved and RAM could just be bluffing. The movement is currently in a quiescent phase. Several of its top leaders have been arrested and others have surrendered. But Honasan, the dissident colonel who is the symbol of RAM, remains underground. He gives occasional interviews threatening yet another coup against Aquino.

Prospects

Aquino's main achievement has been to restore the elite democracy that existed in the Philippines before the Marcos dictatorship. The re-establishment of Congress has meant that the landed elite once again has the institutional means to reconstruct the party-based patronage system. With Marcos gone, patronage has been decentralised and the hierarchy of patron-client relations that existed before martial law, resurrected. The result is an elite-dominated government which is unable and unwilling to address pressing issues of social justice like land redistribution.

Unlike the pre-Marcos era, however, the armed forces are now a major player in politics. Before martial law, military officers were dependent on politicians for patronage and promotions. Although such dependence still exists, politicians aware of the military's power are now more eager to please the AFP. Civilian supremacy remains an uncertain doctrine in the Philippines: there is a fragile balance between civilian and military power, a balance that could tip either way.

The faction of the AFP that has remained loyal to Aquino has played an important role in protecting elite democracy from its challengers within the elite and the armed forces. It has also secured that system against challenges from below, including a peasant-based communist rebellion and grassroots dissent. As in the past, the AFP's main role under Aquino has been in counterinsurgency, a task it has continued to perform with great zeal, despite the strictures of an imperfect democracy.

It is doubtful whether a post-Aquino government will have more success in controlling the AFP. The doctrine of counterinsurgency is so deeply entrenched that any reform of the AFP would require drastic changes. A radical restructuring would inevitably meet bitter opposition within the military and any new government would attempt such reforms at its peril.

Obstacle to democracy

Yet the military remains a major obstacle to the further democratisation of Philippine society. In many parts of the Philippines, the excesses of the military and the civilian elites are checked only by popular organisations which have had some success in campaigning for human rights, land reform, environmental protection and the removal of US bases. But under the guise of counterinsurgency, the AFP have severely repressed grassroots groups challenging the status quo. As a result, these popular movements have been unable to make dramatic progress and their continued existence is threatened by a military paranoia which considers all dissenters as communists.

Because of their involvement in counterinsurgency and the mercenary nature of their activities, including providing protection to criminal syndicates, the AFP are unpopular and any attempt to take over government would meet with popular resistance. A military government would find it difficult to win legitimacy in the Philippines. It would face stiff opposition from popular movements, the politicised clergy and the Catholic Church in general, as well as a middle class accustomed to democratic participation.

But in the short term, the AFP are unlikely to stay out of politics. Patronage networks are as strong as ever in the armed forces and officers remain beholden to elite patrons. In previous Philippine elections, military men have taken an overtly partisan stance, campaigning for politicians as well as providing the guns and muscle to terrorise people to vote for military patrons. The elections in May 1992 will not be any different. In clandestine press conferences, underground RAM leaders have threatened to intervene if the elections are not held to their liking. By late 1991, RAM did not seem to have recovered from the arrests of its leaders and its organisation seemed weaker. But pro-RAM sentiments remain strong among many officers and the possibility of a RAM-led coup cannot be discounted.

A major problem in the Philippines is the lack of countervailing institutions to check the military's power. Congress prefers to court the armed forces rather than confine them to the barracks and has not substantially cut the AFP's size or budget. Nor has it been able to influence counterinsurgency policy. Although congressional committees hold investigations on human rights abuses, they are largely ineffective. Under pressure from the military, the judiciary has upheld the AFP's prerogative to curtail civil liberties. In 1990, for example, the Supreme Court authorised the arrest of suspected 'subversives' without arrest warrants.

Remote peace

The AFP also continue to be the most formidable obstacle to peace negotiations with communist rebels. Although the NDF has expressed its willingness to hold peace talks, the military has objected on the grounds that negotiations would imply recognition of the CPP and the NDF. Talks would violate a fundamental principle of the AFP's counterinsurgency policy: to destroy the legitimacy of the communist movement.

In the long run, a settlement of the NPA rebellion would diminish the AFP's importance. The military's size and budget would have to be drastically cut if there was a peaceful settlement, with military expenditure transferred to more socially useful endeavours. The prospects of ending the rebellion, however, remain remote. The NDF is demanding radical social and political reforms like land redistribution which would hurt the interests of the ruling elites. The Aquino government and its successor are unlikely to implement such reforms, however, thus failing to satisfy the NDF and to persuade NPA guerrillas to lay down their arms.

At the very least, however, negotiations with the rebels could lead to a more humane conduct of the war. The military and the NDF could agree to respect the provisions of the Geneva

Convention, particularly those relating to the protection of civilians and non-combatants, and an independent tribunal could be set up to monitor violations. Such a measure would provide relief to villages which have become the battlefield between the NPA and soldiers. After more than two decades of fighting, many Filipinos would welcome a respite from the brutality of the war.

The armed forces would very likely resist any agreement which would prevent them from fighting the insurgency in the manner to which they have become accustomed. Because the government has not been able to control the AFP, it is up to citizens' groups to stop military abuses. In many parts of the Philippines, popular organisations have made communities aware of their own power, and reduced their vulnerability to the lure of patronage and the threat of violence.

US withdrawal

The next decade is likely to see a reduction of US influence over the Philippines. In September 1991 the Philippine Senate rejected a treaty renewing the American lease of the Subic naval base, one of the largest and most important US overseas military facilities. And in December 1991, the Aquino government negotiated a withdrawal of US troops by the end of 1992. Unless a new Philippine government negotiates another agreement with the United States, the century-long American military presence in the Philippines will come to an end.

Changing global realities, including the break-up of the Soviet Union, have meant the US bases in the Philippines are no longer indispensable to US defence strategy. Although the United States would probably have preferred to stay in the Philippines, the uncertainty of having to negotiate another agreement plus overall cuts in the US budget have reduced the attractiveness of maintaining a presence in the Philippines. While the AFP would also have preferred US troops to stay and exerted strong pressure for a new base treaty, the top brass now seems convinced that the era of US bases has passed.

For Filipinos, the prospect that US troops will withdraw heralds a new beginning. For too long, the United States has been a looming influence over its former colony. The removal of US troops will lessen the need of the US government to interfere in Philippine affairs and to resort to underhanded measures to ensure a pro-US leadership in the country. The closure of Subic base would also mean a cut in US assistance for the Philippine military and would probably weaken pro-American sentiments in the armed forces. As a result, elite-dominated governments no longer able to rely on US patronage might be more willing to concede social reforms in order to maintain their rule in an increasingly restive country. Less US intervention will increase the possibility of democracy growing in the Philippines.

© CIIR
February 1992

Further reading

Final Report of the Fact Finding Commission (into the 1989 Attempted Coup d'État), Bookmark Inc, Manila 1990

M Canlas, M Miranda and J Putzel, *Land, Poverty and Politics in the Philippines*, CIIR 1988

Comment: The Philippines, CIIR 1989

States of Terror: Death Squads or Development?, CIIR 1989

Richard Kessler, *Rebellion and Repression in the Philippines*, Yale University Press, New Haven and London 1989

Kudeta: The Challenge to Philippine Democracy, Philippine Centre for Investigative Journalism, Manila 1990

Factions in the Philippine military, Philippine Resource Centre briefing, April 1990

James Putzel, *A Captive Land: The Politics of Agrarian Reform in the Philippines*, CIIR 1992

James Putzel and John Cunnington, *Gaining Ground: Agrarian Reform in the Philippines*, War on Want Campaigns Ltd 1989

Vigilantes in the Philippines: A Threat to Democratic Rule, Lawyers' Committee for Human Rights, New York 1988

David Wurfel, *Filipino Politics: Development and Decay*, Ateneo de Manila Press, Manila 1988

CIIR *Comment* series

*Comment*s on a range of countries and issues are published regularly by CIIR as contributions to knowledge and debate about current affairs affecting the developing world.

Recent issues include:

Haiti (1988)
Namibia (1989)
Hong Kong (1990)
Angola (1991)

Third World Debt (1991)
Colombia (1992)
Central America (1992)

CIIR

The Catholic Institute for International Relations (CIIR) works to promote justice and development in the Third World. It uses its experience in Latin America, Southern Africa and Asia to produce a range of publications covering development, economics, politics, theology, human rights and social justice.

CIIR members receive a copy of each new issue of *Comment, CIIR News* and other publications. For details of CIIR's activities and membership, write to:

CIIR, Unit 3, Canonbury Yard,
190a, New North Road, London N1 7BJ, United Kingdom
Tel: 071-354 0883 (UK), 4471-354 0883 (international)